Advent 2023
(Dec. 1 — 24)
To Hafez and Hadi
   from Mimi and Papou

This Book is a wonderful story +
a special song.   We will always remember
your visit to Salem when Papou celebrated
  the beginning of his Retirement — with a Party!
Our ^new Little Sailboat is named "Night Owl" —
So we are beginning a new life of our Little Owl.
You two are expecting a new baby brother
   Advent is a Special Time for Expectations + Waiting
and new happenings!   We are sharing a lot
of New Happenings! We Love You! Happy Advent,
                        Mimi + Papou

One Little Owl

Illustrated by Nancy Meyers

ISBN 978-0-9855719-4-8
Printed in Mexico on FSC® paper
from well-managed forests

Music Together LLC
66 Witherspoon Street
Princeton NJ 08542
www.musictogether.com
(800) 728-2692

MUSIC TOGETHER®

One Little Owl

Welcome!

Since 1987, Music Together has been bringing the Joy of Family Music® to young children and their families. This Singalong Storybook offers a new way to enjoy one of our best-loved Music Together songs. We invite you to sing it, read it, and use it as a starting point for conversation and imaginative play with your child.

Using the Book

If you're a Music Together family, you might start singing as soon as you turn the pages. But even if you've never attended one of our classes, you and your child can have hours of fun and learning with this Singalong Storybook. Read the story and enjoy the illustrations with your child, and then try some of the suggested activities that follow. The book can also help inspire artwork or enhance pre-literacy skills. You can even invent your own variations of the story or involve the whole family in some musical dramatic play.

Using the Recording Of course, you will want to have a recording of the song to fully enjoy this book. (See page 31 for how to find Music Together CDs, downloads, and videos about using the books.) And if you play an instrument such as piano or guitar, you'll also find it easy to pick out the song using the music page at the end of the book.

About Music Together®

Music Together classes offer a wide range of activities that are designed to be engaging and enjoyable for children from birth through age seven. By presenting a rich tonal and rhythmic mix as well as a variety of musical styles, Music Together provides children with a depth of experience that stimulates and supports their growing music skills and understanding.

Developed by Founder/Director Kenneth K. Guilmartin and his coauthor, Director of Research Lili M. Levinowitz, Ph.D., Music Together is built on the idea that all children are musical, that their parents and caregivers are a vital part of their music learning, and that their natural music abilities will flower and flourish when they are provided with a sufficiently rich learning environment.

And it's fun! Our proven methods not only help children learn to embrace and express their natural musicality—they often help their grateful grownups recapture a love of music, too. In Music Together classes all over the world, children and their families learn that music can happen anywhere, every day, at any time of the day—and they learn they can make it themselves.

Known worldwide for our mixed-age family classes, we have also adapted our curriculum to suit the needs of infants, older children, and children in school settings such as preschools, kindergartens, and early elementary grades. Visit www.musictogether.com to see video clips of Music Together classes; read about the research behind the program; purchase instruments, CDs, and books; and find a class near you. Keep singing!

About the Song

The song "One Little Owl" is a Music Together favorite that combines so many of the qualities that make our music classes fun. Its haunting melody is in an interesting key; its repetitive quality makes it quickly accessible to children; and its storyline inspires dramatic play. In Music Together classes, children may act out the song—becoming owls, squirrels, crows, and cats that fly, scamper, slink, or swoop onto the tree. Children and their parents can also make up their own verses, putting animals or objects into the tree.

The book adds a dimension that perfectly captures the playfulness of the song. We can witness the increasing plight of the poor old tree as more and more creatures come to sit in its branches—and share in the children's delight as everyone comes (safely) tumbling down.

One little owl said,

whoo whoo

Two little owls said,

whoo whoo

Three little owls said,

whoo whoo

as they sat in
the old oak tree.

One little squirrel said,

sftz sftz sftz

Two little squirrels said,

sftz sftz sftz

13

Three little squirrels said,

sftz sftz sftz

as they sat in
the old oak tree.

One little crow said,
caw caw

Two little crows said,
caw caw

Three little crows said,
caw caw
as they sat in the old oak tree.

One little cat said,

meow
meow

Two little cats said,

meow

meow

18

Three little cats said, meow meow
as they sat in the old oak tree.

One big mommy said, "Hold on tight!"
Two big daddies said, "Hold on tight!"
Three big parents said, "Hold on tight!"

as they sat in the old oak tree.

And the poor old tree said,
"Oh, no!"

The poor old tree said,
"Oh, no!"

The poor old tree said,
"Oh, no!"

"All these things are sitting on me!"

24

Activities

Exploring

Most children like to play with a new book, taking in the pictures a little here, a little there. Some will linger on the pages with squirrels. Others may want to look at the book back to front, or middle to end and back again—and maybe even move and hoot like an owl! Take time to follow your child's inquisitive mind and sense of humor.

Variations

What other animals could sit in the tree? Make up your own version of the song using new animals and their sounds. Ask your child to name an animal—he might think of "monkey," "bear," or "robin"—and then ask him what sound it makes. This can get as silly as you want; for example, what would cows or lions look like in the tree? What sounds would they make? How do they move?

Imagination

Your child may want to put silly or unusual things in the tree: action figures, bicycles, even backhoes or trains! Don't worry, the tree accepts and welcomes all—as long as they're just visiting for a little while.

Literacy

Children delight in making animal sounds. Once the book has become familiar, try singing or saying only the beginnings of the phrases—"one little owl said...," "two little owls said...," etc.—and let your child "read" the sounds that each animal makes as you point to the words. Over time, they will link the sounds they enjoy to the words and letters on the page.

Counting

As each group of animals sits in the tree, you and your child can point to and count them: one, two, three. Over time, your child may enjoy pointing while you count. You can also count the number of acorns or leaves on the tree's various branches. With an older child, you can try counting to higher numbers as more and more animals and people climb onto the tree—there are fifteen at the end!

One Little Owl

Traditional, arranged and adapted
by K. Guilmartin and L. Levinowitz
Additional words by K. Guilmartin

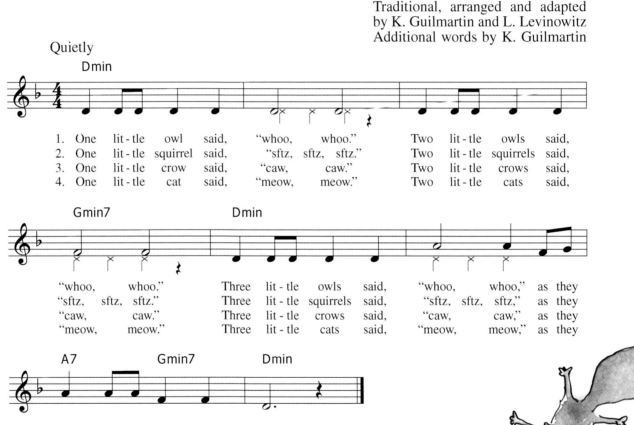

Quietly

Dmin

1. One lit - tle owl said, "whoo, whoo." Two lit - tle owls said,
2. One lit - tle squirrel said, "sftz, sftz, sftz." Two lit - tle squirrels said,
3. One lit - tle crow said, "caw, caw." Two lit - tle crows said,
4. One lit - tle cat said, "meow, meow." Two lit - tle cats said,

Gmin7　　　　　Dmin

"whoo, whoo." Three lit - tle owls said, "whoo, whoo," as they
"sftz, sftz, sftz." Three lit - tle squirrels said, "sftz, sftz, sftz," as they
"caw, caw." Three lit - tle crows said, "caw, caw," as they
"meow, meow." Three lit - tle cats said, "meow, meow," as they

A7　　　Gmin7　　　Dmin

sat in the old oak tree.
sat in the old oak tree.
sat in the old oak tree.
sat in the old oak tree.

Getting the Music

"One Little Owl" has been sung in Music Together classes around the world. It can be found on our award-winning Music Together® **Family Favorites**® CD—available on our website and in select stores and catalogues—and in the Music Together **Tambourine Song Collection** for enrolled families. This song and others are also available for download on our website and on iTunes. To get the most out of your Singalong Storybook, see the videos on our website.

The Family Favorites CD includes 19 songs and a 32-page booklet with many family activities to enjoy. Our award-winning **Family Favorites**® **Songbook for Teachers** features techniques and activities to suit a variety of classroom settings.

Come visit us at **www.musictogether.com**.

31

Music Together LLC

Kenneth K. Guilmartin, Founder/Director

Catherine Judd Hirsch, Director of Publishing and Marketing

Marcel Chouteau, Manager of Production and Distribution

Jill Bronson, Manager of Retail and Market Research

Susan Pujdak Hoffman, Senior Editor

Developed by Q2A/Bill Smith, New York, NY